Old PORTOBELLO

by

Margeorie Mekie

Originally the Free Church, St Philip's Church has stood in Abercorn Terrace, Joppa, since 1877. After the union with the United Presbyterian Church in 1900, the Kirk Session met and agreed to adopt the name of St Philip. This was to honour the Rev. Alexander Philip, during whose ministry the congregation was built up, and whose name and services were remembered with affection. On the evening of Thursday 3 December 1998, a horrendous fire swept through the church, illuminating the cold night skies and totally destroying the roof. The beautiful spire with its one ton bell, and the adjoining hall, where a Brownie meeting was in progress, both miraculously escaped damage.

First published in the United Kingdom, 1999,
by Stenlake Publishing
Telephone / Fax: 01290 551122

ISBN 1 84033 088 0

FURTHER READING

The publications listed below were used by the author during her research. None of them are available from Stenlake Publishing. Those interested in finding out more are advised to contact their local bookshop or reference library.

Annals of Duddingston and Portobello, William Baird.
Third Statistical Account of Scotland.
Edinburgh's Transport, D. L. G. Hunter, 1964.
A Regional History of the Railways of Great Britain, John Thomas, 1971.
Scottish Tramway Fleets, Alan Brotchie, 1968.
Bradshaw's Railway Guide, 2.1.61–5.2.61.
1882 Scottish Gazetteer.
Portobello Golf Club Minute Book.

ACKNOWLEDGEMENTS

When Richard Stenlake approached me and asked if I would consider compiling a book with the help of my collection of Portobello postcards, I was extremely flattered, but rather reluctant to do so as there had already been books written and illustrated on the subject. After many months of pondering, cajoling and bullying by friends, colleagues and family, I was eventually persuaded. I would, however, like to give my special thanks to Robin Baptie for providing the Portobello Amateur Rowing Club photograph and roll of honour, and to Michael Faulds, who photographed the roll of honour; to James Dignall for the photograph of the Eastern Amateur Rowing Club prior to its demolition; to Maggi Dignall who found the birth certificate of Josef Adou; to Walter Hutchison for information about the Portobello Golf Club; to David Jefferies for sharing his wartime experiences and information about the power station; to the staff of Portobello High School; to the Royal Commission on the Ancient and Historical Monuments of Scotland for the picture of the reconstructed power station; to Peter Williamson for his invaluable help on the transport side – the history and identification of tramcars and trains; finally to my husband David, whose help and patience has been invaluable.

INTRODUCTION

Portobello skirts the shores of the River Forth between Leith and Musselburgh, where the Figgate Burn runs into the sea. It was previously known as Land of the Figgate, or The Figgate Whins, and was covered by blown sand, furze, heath, and wild grass, upon which it was said that the monks of Holyrood Abbey used to graze their cattle.

The King's Highway, leading from Edinburgh to the east and south, passed through this wild, desolate region in the Parish of Duddingston, where, until the middle of the eighteenth century not a single dwelling stood. It was a passable road, but by no means safe against highwaymen, especially after sunset.

Portobello took its name from a house built a few years after the 1745 Rebellion. The legend tells of a sailor, George Hamilton, who served with Admiral Vernon's fleet of six warships which successfully bombarded and captured the Spanish town of Puerto Bello on the Isthmus of Panama. The Spanish port had been a source of danger to British shipping. The attack was made in November 1739 when a great amount of gold, gun ammunition and other valuables fell into the hands of the victors. It would appear that Hamilton retired from naval life following this incident, and took a fancy for the wilderness beside the sea on the Firth of Forth. He built himself a solitary cottage which he named 'Portobello', and settled down to spend the rest of his days in the shoe and harness-making trade. The monthly stage-coach between Edinburgh and London travelled along the road, and there was also passing foot trade – fisherwomen from Musselburgh with their baskets or creels loaded with fish, and salters from Joppa and Pinkie Pans, all on their way to Edinburgh to ply their trade. George Hamilton converted his cottage to provide refreshments for weary travellers. He must have anticipated a healthy business, being a halfway house between Edinburgh and Musselburgh.

Some time around 1763 William Jameson, later to become known as the 'Father of Portobello', discovered a valuable bed of clay near the Figgate Burn and erected the first brick and tile works on the banks of the stream (he subsequently built an earthenware factory there too). These works gave rise to a small village, and as other works were established the village swelled into a small town. By the end of the nineteenth century there were not only potteries and brickworks, but an extensive paper works in Bridge Street owned by brothers Alfred and Frank Nichol. This employed some eighty men, women and girls.

At the end of the eighteenth century the beauty of the beach, the fineness of the sands, and its suitability as a bathing place began to draw the attention of the citizens of Edinburgh to Portobello, and thereafter many neat dwelling houses and villas for the accommodation of summer visitors were built, transforming the town into a fashionable watering place.

Much to the sadness of many of the citizens of Portobello, this little town was amalgamated with Edinburgh in 1896.

THE TRAMWAY SYSTEM

In 1904, the Musselburgh & District Electric Light and Traction Company opened an electric tramway system from Musselburgh to Joppa, where it connected with the Edinburgh cable system. Further extension in the opposite direction took place in 1909, when the rails reached Port Seton. Because of the different types of traction, no through running was possible, and passengers had to change trams at Joppa if they were travelling from the Musselburgh area to Portobello or Edinburgh.

In 1919 Edinburgh Corporation took over the cable system and by 1923 had converted it to electricity (the Portobello line was the last to be changed), so that changing trams at Joppa was no longer necessary.

The Musselburgh company abandoned the section of their line from Levenhall to Port Seton in 1928, and in 1931 the Edinburgh Corporation acquired the line from Joppa to Levenhall. (The Musselburgh company continued to operate buses through Portobello under the fleet name 'Coast Line' until its take-over by the Scottish Motor Traction Company in 1936.) Electric trams remained in service on various routes through Portobello until the 1950s, when bus services gradually replaced them. Tram services to Portobello finally ceased on 10 July 1956. A new bus depot was built at the Marine Gardens, and opened in 1962.

Portobello Station was opened in 1846, at the same time as the North British Railway main line from Edinburgh to Berwick-upon-Tweed, and was rebuilt in 1887 with an island platform. In the early years of the twentieth century Portobello was a busy suburban station, and for the period from July to December 1920 no less than 431,559 passengers used it. In 1961, towards the end of its days, a number of services still stopped at the station including some of the Edinburgh to Berwick local services; trains from Edinburgh to Peebles; from Edinburgh to Carlisle via Galashiels on the 'Waverley' route; and local services on the Edinburgh south side circle. A through service between Corstorphine and North Berwick, calling at Portobello approximately every hour, also ran at that time. With improvements to road transport services, however, passenger numbers declined, and on 7 September 1964 the station closed, along with nearby Joppa.

The Cock o' the North fast train from Edinburgh to Berwick passing through Portobello Station.

The golf clubhouse was opened in June 1911, and apart from having had electricity installed has remained essentially unchanged. It is in Stanley Street, backing on to the railway line, and overlooking the golf course. The beautiful semi-circular stone steps lead up to a balcony where benches are to be found. Amongst the trophies in Portobello Golf Club's possession is the Harry Lauder Trophy, presented by Sir Harry himself on Saturday 20 June 1924. This trophy was competed for by members in connection with the Individual Championships, a very popular event which always attracted a large entry. However, with a decline in membership and in order to stimulate more interest, the trophy became an open event in 1979.

The *Golfers Handbook* of 1936 included Portobello amongst the oldest golf clubs, giving the year of institution as 1856, although a golfing annual of 1886/1887 quotes the much later year of 1883, when ex-Provost Wood was captain. At that time the golf course was in Joppa in an area known locally as The Quarry. The course shown here was created in 1908, and although play continued throughout the First World War, the land was put under cultivation during the years 1939 to 1945 and the course was not reopened until 1953. In recent years it has undergone various alterations: bunkers have been improved, the rough has been left to grow between the course and the football pitches to the south, and new trees have been planted, making this a very pretty little nine-hole course.

Stanley Street School was located on the road leading to the golf club. It was a small school, run by Miss Shiells, with a roll of some forty to fifty boys and girls. It first appears in the street directory in 1899. This picture is thought to have been taken about 1901.

In 1912 the premises of Miss Shiells' school were purchased by the Baptist Church. This picture gives a clear view of the street, public park and golf course that the former school overlooked. By 1922 the Baptist Church had moved again, this time to 189 Portobello High Street, the site of Portobello's first house.

The Burgh School opened in 1876 with a roll of almost 300 pupils, and had more than doubled this number by 1881. However, in the latter years of the nineteenth century epidemics such as diphtheria and scarlet fever, combined with poor attendance, greatly reduced the numbers in each class. By 1901 the Higher Grade Department had been established, and the school roll gradually expanded again, with local children able to receive a secondary education. In 1964 a new comprehensive school was built to accommodate more than 1,550 pupils. Apart from the eight storeys of classrooms, it had a swimming pool plus workshops and laboratories with all the latest equipment. The old school continued to be used as an annexe until the school roll once again fell. Today, builders have converted the old school building into two- and three-bedroomed flats.

Portobello School hockey team posing outside the school. The headmaster, Mr William MacKay, stands in the middle of the photograph at the back. First assistant, Mr David Clark Thomson Mekie, geography teacher, is at the right-hand side of the photograph. The picture was probably taken before the First World War, prior to Mr Mekie enlisting for War Service. There would appear to be eleven members of the team and four reserves. Could the one boy have been the team mascot?

Lee Crescent was named after the lawyer who originally owned the land that it was built on. The typical seaside holiday shop is full of souvenirs, toys to tempt the children, and postcards for visitors to buy and send off to their friends and relatives. This one was sent to Ireland in 1913. The sender remarks on the lovely time she is having at Portobello! The scene has not changed much, although the streets are now lined with parked cars and for some time the shop has been a hairdressing salon.

A busy turn of the century street scene (the postcard was sent in 1902). The location is the crossroads of Portobello High Street with Bath Street leading off to the left and Brighton Place, just out of the picture, to the right. The earliest forms of public transport in the Edinburgh area were horse-drawn omnibuses and coaches, and in the 1860s there was an hourly service from Edinburgh to Portobello. In 1871 a steam-driven bus was introduced, but due to the poor state of the roads it only operated for a short time. The Edinburgh Street Tramways Company was incorporated in 1871, and proposed a service to and from Portobello, but it was 1875 before the line was built and services started from Waterloo Place. A small tram shed was built at Rosefield Place. Various experiments with steam trams took place in the 1870s and 1880s, but none were successful. Powers to introduce cable traction were obtained in 1893, and in 1894 the Edinburgh and District Tramway Company took over as operator. A cable service started in 1902. The long cables were suspended in a slot between the running rails, and the trams were controlled by a 'gripper' operated by the driver. The cables were driven by steam engines, and an engine for the Portobello line was installed in a depot on Portobello High Street.

The building with the clock on the right housed Portobello's first cinema-theatre, where silent movies were shown accompanied by a lone pianist thumping away at the piano. This was the former site of George Hamilton's cottage, which had been demolished in 1862. Following its removal, work commenced on a town hall which was to include council offices, plus a hall for public entertainments such as concerts, soirees, and lectures. The hall later became the Star Cinema. Windsor Place United Free Church is in the centre of the picture.

The original town hall premises proved to be inadequate for municipal purposes, and a suitable site for a new building was purchased on the north side of the High Street adjoining Ramsay Lane. In 1878 a magnificent building in Scottish Baronial style was ready for occupation. There were offices for the town clerk, treasurer and registrar, with police cells and accommodation for the horse-drawn fire engine at the rear. The tower was fitted with a clock and bell. The building still functions as the local police station today.

This site in Bath Street was previously occupied by a variety hall belonging to the well-known artiste André Letta, who laid on various entertainments for the benefit of holidaymakers. Following the hall's demolition, the County Cinema was built in its place, opening on 30 March 1939 with *Snow White and the Seven Dwarfs* and *Air Devils*. The auditorium walls were notable for their art deco lines, and outside neon tubes illuminated the central tower in constantly-changing colours. In 1954 the cinema was reconstructed and became the George. It was intended to be a 'festival cinema', and hoped to draw in sophisticated crowds from the Edinburgh Festival. The cinema closed its doors on Saturday 15 June 1974 and the building is now used as a bingo hall.

In 1902, no. 26 Bath Street (the small domed building on the left) was modestly described as 'A Hall with Lavatories'. The American Wilbur Harlan converted this one-time roller-skating rink into a handsome cinema (*c.*1912), picturesquely named the Bungalow Electric Theatre, which he ran with the help of his son. He made several alterations to the building, including adding the cupola and an entrance kiosk. It later passed into the hands of the Forth Cinema Company, Glasgow, who owned it until its closure on 26 May 1956. By this time it was known as the Victory Cinema, having changed its name in 1942. The last film to be shown was *John and Julie*, starring Moira Lister and Constance Cummings.

On 1 October 1912 Maurice Harlan, cinematograph operator, aged 23, and Mary Gray Campbell, aged 20, were married by James Oliver, Minister of St James's Church Portobello, at Argyle House in Hope Lane. Mr Harlan's father was the proprietor of the Bungalow Electric Theatre in Bath Street. The picture shows the happy couple and their guests eager to tuck into the sandwiches, crumpets, scones and wedding cake that have been laid on. The compulsory wedding photographs, to remind them of the joyful occasion, have to be taken first though!

In 1914, in view of the sustained increase in demand for electricity, Edinburgh Corporation decided to purchase property which would become the site of a new power station. This was at the junction of Kings Road and Portobello High Street. The River Forth lay immediately to the north, thus ensuring an unlimited supply of cooling water, and the site was also conveniently located for delivery of fuel from the Lothian coalfields. Construction was delayed by the First World War, but in the spring of 1919 the pre-war plans were revived and by 1920 a power station, on a much larger scale than originally anticipated, was in the process of being built. Originally built with three stubby chimneys, a fourth was added later. The first section of the Portobello Power Station was officially opened by HM King George V on 11 July 1923.

Portobello residents living nearby complained about the amount of smoke produced by the coal-fired power station, but despite this it was extended. The four small chimneys were replaced by one tall stack, and a second opening ceremony was held on Wednesday 20 April 1930. Portobello Power Station was demolished in 1980, and power is now supplied by Cockenzie Power Station and the atomic facility at Torness near Dunbar. A fellow postcard collector, David Jefferies, remembers the power station during the Second World War: 'During the first air raid on mainland Britain, several German planes attacked the Forth Rail Bridge and naval ships at Rosyth, but were dispersed by Hurricanes from Turnhouse Airport. At that time we lived on the lower slopes of Arthur's Seat, and we had an excellent view of a German plane flying low and trying to escape from a pursuing fighter. It went low over the coast and tried to draw the Hurricane onto the chimney of Portobello Power Station. At the last moment it side-slipped round the chimney with the fighter going round the other side. All the time orange flashes could be seen from the tail of the bomber and from the fighter. The Hurricane finally got its target further down the coast. I was a schoolboy at that time and I joined many others by cycling down to Portobello to try and pick up spent bullets. They were hot, and many a mother wondered why her beloved son's handkerchief had holes burnt in it!'

This picture, taken inside Portobello Power Station, is thought to show the drive shaft for one of the turbines.

The Marine Gardens were opened in 1910 on a beautiful site by the shores of the River Forth. They were a Mecca for pleasure seekers from all over the United Kingdom, and the variety of entertainment on offer was unsurpassed. The gardens were created by a group of businessmen, who got the idea from the 1908 Scottish National Exhibition held in Saughton Park. They arranged for many of the elaborate buildings to be transported from the temporary exhibition site at Saughton to this more permanent location on the shores of the Forth.

Capt. Sadler,
Zoo Director and Wild Animal Trainer, Edinburgh Marine Park and Zoological Gardens, Portobello

Capt. Sadler with the lion cubs "Wallace" and "Bruce," born Marine Zoological Gardens, May 14th, 1911.

One of the most popular attractions at the Marine Park was the Zoological Gardens, which housed one of the finest collections of wild animals in Scotland. There were over sixty cages and the animals on display included elephants, lions, tigers, wolves, hyenas and monkeys. On 14 May 1911, lion cubs were born at the Marine Gardens. They were given the Scottish names of Wallace and Bruce.

The Marine Gardens even contained a Somali village. The villagers were from the Khadaboursi Tribe of Djibouti, and on 29 July 1910 a son was born to the chief of the tribe. It is a great tribute to the town that the chief named his son 'Josef Cuabri Portobello Adou'.

The Marine Gardens were a fun seekers paradise, and young and old could spend many hours of amusement there. Diversions included the river caves, aeroplanes, mountain slide, royal mountain scenic railway, katzenjammer castle, great joy wheel, Parker's shooting range, and for the not-so-lily-livered the figure eight railway. Each car held twenty-eight people and the switchback was three tiers high. The run took between four and five minutes, and on the dip the car travelled at approximately fifty miles per hour. The track, which was one mile long, was illuminated with over 3,000 electric light bulbs.

The Empress Ballroom was the largest and most elaborate ballroom in Scotland with a perfect floor which could accommodate 2,000 dancers. This postcard shows it being used as a roller-skating rink. During the First World War it became a dormitory for soldiers. The message on the back of this undated card begins 'Here is a postcard of the place we sleep in as it used to be'. Another card, showing the exterior of the skating hall, dated 1 November 1913, bears the message 'Just a postcard of my billet. This is an eye opener in the Winter Gardens Portobello in front of the sea.'

A group of Royal Scots posing outside the concert hall. Soldiers were not strangers to the Marine Gardens, and in happier times before the outbreak of war, military bands, such as the Royal Scots Greys and the Irish Fusiliers, had played in the band court, ballroom and theatre.

The Concert Hall was originally one of the noted features of the Scottish National Exhibition of 1908 which had been held in the grounds of Saughtonhall Park, Edinburgh. Along with other buildings from Saughtonhall it was re-erected on the site of the Marine Gardens. It was a most striking building – circular in shape with ornately decorated outside walls. The roundness was relieved by four ornamental towers which gave access to the gallery inside. The hall could accommodate 3,000 people. Hibbert's 'High-Class Moving Pictures' were shown every afternoon, and, in the evenings, star artistes entertained both young and old with 'Vaudeville Turns'.

Portobello Bathing Pool cost £90,000 to build and was opened on Saturday 30 May 1936. This beautiful art deco building stood on what had previously been the site of the Rosebank Potteries. There was accommodation for 6,000 spectators who enjoyed diving displays, races and floodlit evening galas. One of the main features was the wave machine which could produce three-foot high waves, giving a realistic imitation of sea-breakers, much to the delight of the bathers. During the war the swimming pool was camouflaged with a covering of netting so that it resembled a grassy field, as it presented a guide for bombers to the adjacent power station. The pool reopened in 1946 for the summer season after six years of closure.

Few of Scotland's outdoor swimming pools have survived, and Portobello's is no exception. Tourists are now travelling abroad to warmer climates where they can bask in Mediterranean sunshine instead of shivering at British resorts. In 1980 Portobello's outdoor pool closed its doors, and for nearly a decade it remained a derelict eyesore. Eventually the site was purchased and today there are eight five-a-side football pitches with a modern pavilion. A building for indoor bowls overlooks the sea.

The Fun City amusement park was located next to the outdoor bathing pool. This picture shows its figure eight railway (not to be confused with the one at the Marine Gardens) and helter skelter. Inside the park there was a waltzer, swings, roundabouts, and dodgems, which were always very popular. Loud music filled the air and gaily coloured lights flashed on and off. There were side shows and many a child could be seen joyfully clutching a prized plastic bag containing a poor goldfish swimming around in circles. In 1957 the figure eight was dismantled, having been condemned as too dangerous. The tiny outlet tunnel on the right of the picture, situated between Fun City and the open air swimming pool, is where the Figgate Burn flows out to the sea. The area in the foreground was once the location of a pier and harbour, built *c.*1788 to meet the requirements of importing coal, whiteware clay from Cornwall and other commodities for the growing industries of Portobello. However, the basin was small and the entrance to the harbour narrow. Sixty years later the pier was in ruins, the basin filled with sand, and the harbour had become a haven for small boys and their toy boats.

Photo by Low,] THE GEISHA ENTERTAINERS, **HARBOUR GREEN PAVILION, PORTOBELLO.** [*Portobello.*
HARRY MARVELLO, *Sole Proprietor.*

In 1905, Harry Marvello arrived in Portobello with his concert party, The Geisha Entertainers. He had spent the previous season entertaining visitors at Ayr. Harry built a large stage and dressing room on Harbour Green, where the Fun City was later erected. With his sister Alice at the piano and the entertainers smartly turned out in naval jackets, white drill trousers and caps, they were an immediate success and crowds turned out in abundance to watch their open air performances. Harry made sure that his programme was varied frequently and his Geishas entertained the public with songs, sketches and energetic dances. Talent contests were also held with the winner receiving a gold medallion.

A signed postcard of pierrot Trelvin Wayne, dated 18 August 1907. The card is addressed to his sweetheart, and reminds her of their date the following Monday. Trelvin Wayne was a member of a troupe called Melville's Royal Pierrots, who were playing at the pavilion on Portobello Pier at the time.

Portobello pier cost £10,000 to build and was opened on 23 May 1871. It was designed by the Englishman Thomas Bouch, who had been the engineer of the ill-fated first Tay Bridge, which collapsed in 1870 while a train was crossing the River Tay. The pier extended 1,250 feet into the sea and was 22 feet broad, increasing to 60 feet at the head which was surmounted by a pavilion. It was a calling place for day excursions, and the steps that led up to the entrance kiosk had boards with posters advertising the list of sailing trips for the day. Storms caused much damage to the pier, requiring heavy and frequent expenditure on structural repair. This led to its closure and eventual removal.

The head of the pier was constructed from timbers supported on iron piles. There was a pavilion with a restaurant and concert hall, and a small camera obscura projected beautiful views of the River Forth and the winding shores of the Fife coast. Steamers from the Galloway Steam Packet Company were regular callers at the pier, conveying pleasure-seekers to the historic Bass Rock, the Island of May and, for the more adventurous, to such far away places as St Andrews. The destinations of the steamers were published every day in the morning newspapers.

For many years Portobello beach was looked on as being an excellent exercise ground for the cavalry who were stationed at the nearby Piershill Barracks. The Royal Scots Greys and the 16th and 17th Lancers were all known to bring their horses down to the sands. In the early years of the nineteenth century, the Volunteer Cavalry Regiment came from their headquarters in Musselburgh to exercise their horses here, and Sir Walter Scott used to delight in walking his big black horse up and down the beach.

Piershill Barracks, on the Portobello Road, where the regimental horses were stabled. The spacious barracks were built in 1793 using stones excavated from the quarry at Craigmillar. They could accommodate two regiments of cavalry, and formed three sides of a quadrangle, the fourth side being a high wall in which two large gateways were set.

An 1899 photograph showing the first section of Marlborough Mansions to be built. This very superior block of flats included balconies enclosed by intricately designed iron railings, with the odd green conifer standing on them. The entrance to the flats was on the promenade and the ground floor accommodated ice-cream parlours and cafes, plus shops selling souvenirs and those long thin sticks of candy wrapped in cellophane. These, of course, were the sticks of rock that no seaside resort was complete without. The interior of the white rock contained red lettering spelling out the word 'Portobello'.

Right: One of the shops below Marlborough Mansions, the elegant flats beside the pier. The address is no. 34, Promenade, the year is 1911, and the shop is celebrating the June Coronation of King George V and Queen Mary. Not only does it advertise the sale of tea, sandwiches and cigarettes, but buckets and spades can be seen hanging up in the doorway.

Two contrasting photographs of Marine Parade, Portobello. The parade was part of the promenade, and the photographs were taken by a Paisley photographer, Mr John B. Martin, in June 1899. Perhaps he had come to Portobello for a holiday beside the sea, and had decided to combine business with pleasure. The daytime picture shows a few people enjoying themselves on the sands, with others strolling along the promenade. The night-time photograph was taken at 10.30 p.m., and shows the bathing huts beached high up on the sand, whilst the washing that was hung out earlier has been taken in. Lamplighters, commonly known as 'leeries', had to light the gas lamps by hand.

A later photograph of the promenade, taken after the pier was demolished, with Marlborough Mansions towering in the background. The Prince of Wales drinking fountain at the foot of Wellington Street (now Marlborough Street) still stands today, but no longer functions as a fountain. André Letta, who had previously owned a variety hall in Bath Street, set up his large tent on this section of the promenade at the bottom of Wellington Street. Donald Peers entertained at André Letta's Pavilion while he was a serviceman stationed at Piershill Barracks. He was just one of many up-and-coming stars to begin his career with one of these popular troupes of seaside entertainers.

The bathing machine first arrived in Portobello in the summer of 1795. It was a coach raised well above the sand by four large wheels, with a flight of six wooden steps leading to the door. The bather entered the coach, which was then harnessed to a horse which pulled it into the sea until the water level rose to the fourth or fifth step. The horse was then freed and led back to the beach to go through the same performance for its next customer. Having donned his or her costume, the bather would then modestly open the doors of the bathing machine and take the plunge. On completion of the exercise, one end of a towel was pushed through a small porthole at the back of the machine as a signal to the attendant that he should return with his horse and pull it back to its stance on the sands.

The original post office was in the High Street and was run by Mr James Newlands. Delivering correspondence during the early part of the nineteenth century was not an onerous task, and Mr Newlands, who was an important local businessman, also operated as house agent, valuator, banker, auctioneer, and wine importer. He employed a post runner – a widow named Nanny Moffat – who discharged her duties with faithfulness, and was apparently a great favourite among the inhabitants of the village. As Portobello prospered, however, the post office had to move, and was transferred to these premises in Windsor Place. Times have changed and post offices have now been relocated in small shops or large supermarkets. Portobello's is no exception, and Windsor Place Post Office has closed to the public, although today the premises continue to function as a sorting office.

Portobello Sea Water Baths were erected by the Corporation and opened in 1901. The baths were highly recommended by doctors for patients who were suffering from rheumatism, sciatica and nervous disorders. For a moderate charge visitors could plunge into the swimming pool or relax in the luxury of a Turkish or Russian bath. There was an ornamental balcony for spectators to watch the swimmers and another balcony over the entrance of the baths where visitors could enjoy the splendid view of the neighbouring coastline and watch children making sandcastles on the beach. The Salvation Army enticed holidaymakers and locals to join in their hymn-singing on a Sunday at the foot of Melville Street next to the baths, before handing round their collecting tins hoping for generous donations.

The Portobello Amateur Rowing Club was formed in the early 1870s and its oarsmen could regularly be seen out on the River Forth. This postcard, dated 1903, shows boats taking part in the Portobello Regatta passing the end of the pier. Each boat contained four oarsmen and a cox. Many smaller boats turned out to watch the occasion. At one time Portobello supported two rowing clubs, The Portobello Amateur Rowing Club on the promenade, and The Eastern Amateur Rowing Club, round the corner in Pittville Street. Today neither exist. Through neglect and possibly lack of funds, the wooden clubhouse at the foot of Pittville Street became an unsightly ruin, and has now been replaced by a tasteful block of flats. In summer, where there were once rowing boats, power boats now skim across the water pulling enthusiastic water-skiers behind them. Promenaders are also entertained by the sedate yachts that venture forth from Fisherrow Harbour.

Members of the Portobello Amateur Rowing Club pose in their Sunday best during the 1913 season. The badges on the boater hats show crossed oars with the initials P.A.R.C. The members are, from left to right:

Back row: W. R. McNiven, J. Matthews, H. O. Cook, G. V. Gray and A .A. Brown.
Third Row: J. A. G. Lorimer, P. W. Leslie, A. Carmichael, P. B. Care, H. Wrightson and J. E. A. Turnbull.
Second Row: E. Muir, F. M. Calder (who died while fighting for his country during the Great War), J. Burnet (Lieut.), A. D. Kellock (Captain), L. J. Brown (President), R. Flockhart (Secretary), A. J. Lyall (Treasurer) and D. McNie.
Front Row: F. Brand, C. Davidson, T. Willis and C. B. Stewart – all proudly holding the rudders!

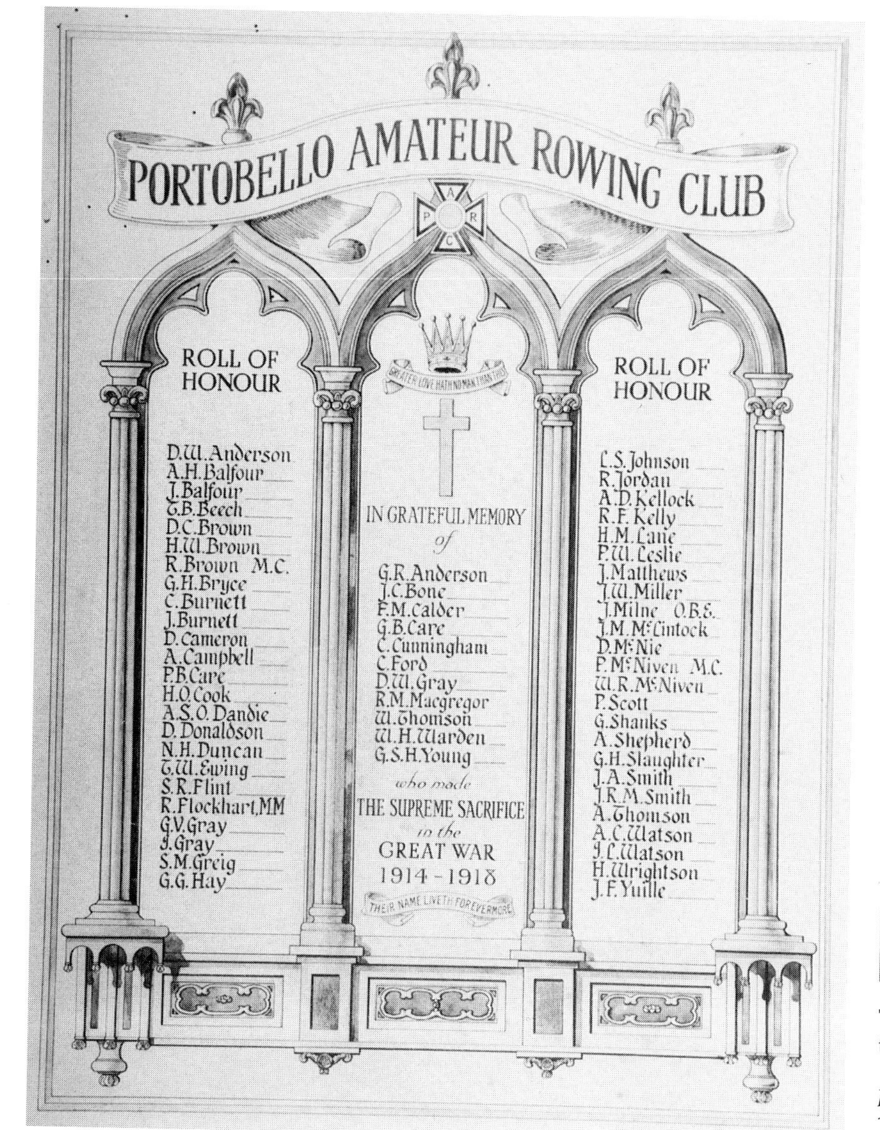

The Eastern Amateur Rowing Club premises in Pittville Street, prior to their demolition.

Left: The Portobello Amateur Rowing Club roll of honour from the 1914-1918 war.

A permanent bandstand and shelters, located on the corner of John Street and the promenade, were built by the town council and opened for public use on 1 June 1906. The shelters surrounded the band on three sides, leaving the promenade side open so that others could watch or listen while walking by or sitting on the sands. Owing to inclement weather and lack of maintenance, the area fell into disrepair, but after refurbishment in the summer of 1960 the site was reopened to the public. The bandstand was replaced by a children's paddling pool. The original shelters were demolished and replaced by a new shelter on the promenade side. Although perhaps not pretty to look at, it did keep the cold north winds out while parents sat and watched their children splashing in the water. The shelter and the paddling pool are still there, although nowadays the pool is never filled with water.

This building, previously known as Easter Duddingston Lodge, was once owned by the Duke of Abercorn. In 1858 it was leased to Mr Charles Jenner, who purchased it in November 1874 and had it reconstructed and enlarged. Mr Jenner was the proprietor of 'Jenner's Departmental Store' in Princes Street. He used the lodge as accommodation for staff, and many 'Jenner's girls' stayed there. Twenty years later, in 1894, Easter Duddingson Lodge came back on the market. It was described as being a dwelling house surrounded by trees, enclosed within high stone walls, with magnificent views from the front across the Forth to the shores of Fife and the Lomond Hills.

The new owners of Easter Duddingston Lodge opened its doors to the public as the luxurious Queen's Bay Hotel. Apart from the putting green, its magnificent grounds included a 'bridge in the wilderness', and very fine rockery gardens. It was an ideal holiday location where one could walk in the beautifully laid out gardens, relax in the shade of the large trees, or take a stroll along the sea front where the air was clean and fresh – and extremely bracing in the winter months.

The entrance to the Queen's Bay Hotel on the Milton Road, the old route of the A1 from Edinburgh to Musselburgh. The road has now been widened considerably, and the house on the right demolished. The railing on the left is known as the Scaligar Railing, and was made in 1890 at Portobello by James Ross, blacksmith, and his assistant, David Greig. It is an exact replica of the Scaligar Railing at Verona in Italy. On another postcard showing a picture of the railing, written in 1908, the writer states 'We are having a lovely time here. The railings in this picture are a curio. They are all in wee bits. You can shake it and it shakes all over.'

This paddling pool was situated at the end of the promenade at Joppa. It was located near the rocks where parents could sit and relax in the sun while keeping an eye on their offspring splashing around gleefully. During the early 1970s the ever-diminishing sand was pumped back on to the beach, and, until recently, only a few stones poked their noses up from it. Children can still be seen with their buckets exploring the rock pools, seeking crabs and tiny fish which have been marooned in the pools by the ebbing tide.

This card was posted in Edinburgh on 16 March 1909 and shows a group of Africans enjoying themselves on the sands at Joppa. The chimneys of the Joppa Salt Pans can be seen in the background, and a few local people have gathered to witness this uncommon scene. But who are they? Was the photograph taken in 1908, during the time of the Scottish National Exhibition? Could they be from Somaliland, and be giving Portobello the once-over before setting up their village at the Marine Gardens in 1910? They certainly look very imposing in their long white robes.

Tramway traffic became very heavy in the summer months when visitors flocked to the seaside. This postcard shows Edinburgh & District Tramways Co. tramcar No. 169 standing at the terminal stub before making its return journey to the post office in Waterloo Place. In the background, passengers are alighting from tram No. 100 which will cross over to the return rail once No. 169 leaves. The groove for the cable can be clearly seen between the running lines. These two trams were part of a batch which entered service between 1899 and 1901 and were built by Brown Marshall in Birmingham. Both were later taken over by Edinburgh Corporation and converted to run on electricity. They were also fitted with roofs for the upper decks.

Musselburgh & District tram No. 9 at the Joppa terminus, about to depart for Levenhall. This was one of ten trams built in 1904 at the British Electric Car Company's works at Trafford Park, Manchester. An Edinburgh & District cable car stands behind it. When new, the Musselburgh trams were painted red and ivory, although some were later repainted green. The colour scheme of the Edinburgh trams was officially described as 'madder and white', the colours used to this day by Lothian Region Transport.